Laughing Camera for Children

Photographs

Laughing Camera for Children

Edited by Hanns Reich

HILL AND WANG · NEW YORK
A Division of Farrar, Straus & Giroux

think water and the beach hold many fond memories for all of us.

3

4

I know you don't like kittens, but isn't this one cute?

ou think
n messy,
an you
magine
f you had
of these?

appreciation
e what you
ave is what
ounts.!

I told you
I would
teach
you how
to dance

12

15

check out
this
pose!!

"New York City, just like I pictured it!"

We never saw that at the Bronx Zoo!!

You think you have problems!

Driving is a
blast
specially
when
our
Doday
teachs
you
how!

(this doesn't
look like
green acres
parking
lot)

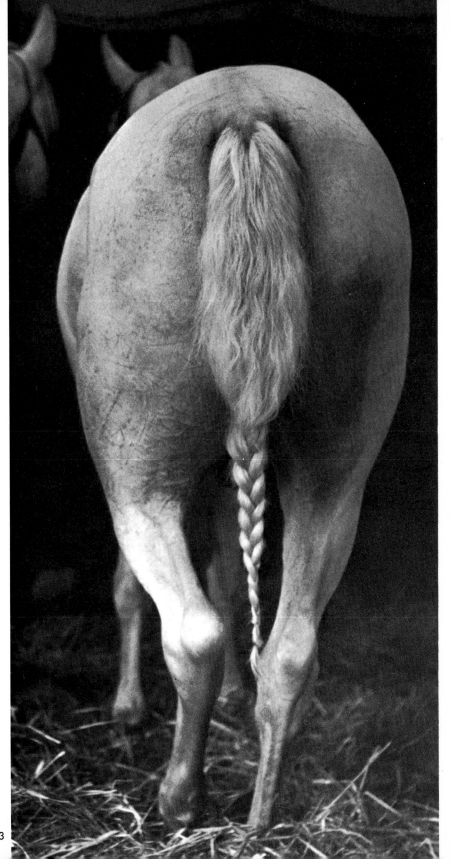

33

I guess everyone reads the newspaper!

Do you remember the time Yvonne and I played this game?
yes, I walked into a wall.'

laurens,
dog
nuffin!!

You think
you have
it
Rough?

You must be wondering now what relation this book has on your 40th birthday. There comes a time in everyone's life where one must sit back and relax. I am seeing that clearer and clearer everyday. Take a deep breath, no that's not deep enough — hold it, longer, now let go a slowly. Drop those shoulders!! Doesn't that feel better? Look at the picture to the left. If one becomes too serious, you may end up like this.

Enjoyment is a very special part of life. Sure, Responsibility has it's ifs, ands and buts but I guess in order to reach enjoyment R you must upkeep those responsibilities. You are responsible so now enjoy yourself, especially today.

Daddy, you've taught me so much in the past 18 years. Everything from drinking out of a bottle to being independent. I thank you a million times.

$\longrightarrow$

I love you very much and I only hope today
and tommorrow and the next etc. are happy ones.

"Happy Birthday".

"Children's children are the crown of old men;
and the glory of children are their fathers."

Proverbs 17:6

P.S
See you
soon!!

All my love always